DISCOVER
UK DIVING

RED FLANNEL PUBLISHING

Published in 2010 by Red Flannel Publishing,
Plumtree House, Mill Lane, East Runton, Norfolk,
NR27 9PH

Printed by Barnwell Print Ltd, Aylsham, Norfolk

Designed by Jo Cole
www.clearsoundandvision.com

Photographs copyright - Will Appleyard
All the underwater photographs in this book were
taken with a compact Canon IXUS 860IS, INON
wide angle lens & Sea & Sea strobe.

The right of Will Appleyard to be identified as
the author of this work has been asserted by him
in accordance with the Copyright, Designs and
Patent Act 1988

ISBN 978-0-9561346-3-9

Scuba diving can be dangerous; this book should
be used simply as dive site guide. The divers
safety ultimately lays with the diver him or herself.

www.divinguk.co.uk

CONTENTS

DISCOVER UK DIVING

Featuring five southern counties

CORNWALL

DEVON

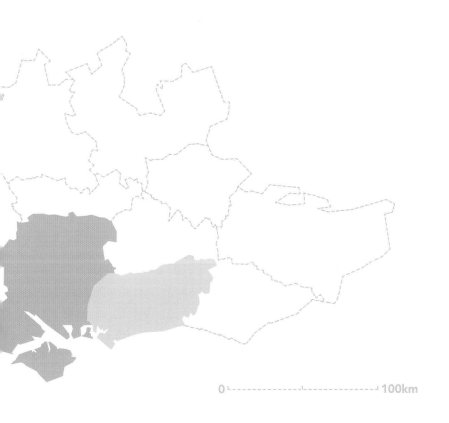

0 ⌊------------⌊------------⌋ 100km

DORSET

HAMPSHIRE

WEST SUSSEX

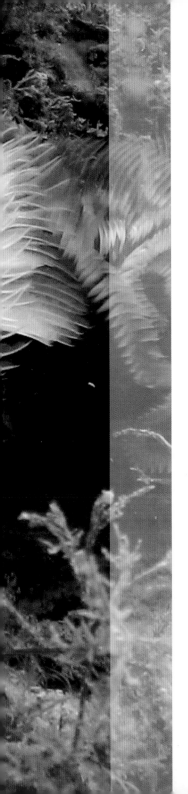

Inroduction

Discover UK diving is a personal guide geared towards those wishing to explore some of the most accessible and popular dive sites surrounding our stunning coast, but perhaps don't know where to start.

I have included just a few of my favourite sites across five southern counties and hope that my suggestions will inspire others to explore what is lurking beneath. There are literally hundreds of dive sites around the UK and in this book and I have covered just a handful to get you going.

Playful seals, coral and sponges, curious crustaceans, enormous eels and wartime wrecks – it is all there waiting to be discovered.

Get stuck in...

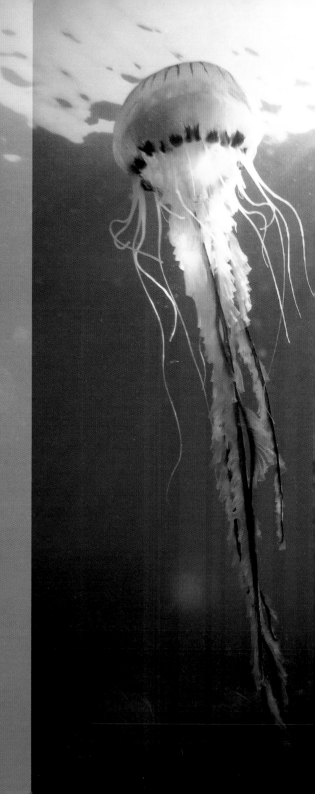

FEATURED DESTINATIONS

IANTD CERTIFICATED IDE N° 2 B

Dry suits and wet suits

Diving in UK waters requires more in the way of equipment to protect you against the elements, compared to the kit you might need when diving in warmer climates.

The temperature of the sea can range from around six to twenty degrees, depending on the time of year. If you intend to dive all year round in this country, then be prepared to invest in a dry suit and good quality under suit. In summer months, especially mid to late summer when the water temperature has reached its peak, a semi dry suit or thick wet suit will be more than adequate for a 30 – 40 minute dive within 20 metres of water. Below that depth you will become chilly quite quickly. That said, it is not uncommon to see divers in wet suits during winter months too. With both types of exposure suite, a hood and gloves will also be essential, although I regularly dive without both items during the summer months. They are both essential in winter and gloves will not just offer protection against the cold, they will also prevent cuts and scrapes to your water softened hands when diving on wrecks.

Surface Marker Buoy (SMB)

 If you invest in nothing else, and hire all your diving equipment, it is imperative that you become proficient in the use of a surface marker buoy or "SMB". In most cases, as part of the boat briefing, the majority of skippers will ensure that each diver is in possession of an SMB and is familiar with its use.

Many dives off our coast can involve a drift at some point, so the only way the boat's skipper will be able to follow his divers will be by the presence of SMB's on the surface. On a drift dive, usually one member of a buddy pair or small group will be asked to send up their buoy when they reach the seabed. Should you become separated from your buddy or group, you will also be required to deploy a marker buoy, or at the very least be in possession of a signalling device for use at the surface, for example a dive flag. Ideally you should seek additional SMB training, or practice in controlled conditions before embarking on an open water dive in the UK, if not already confident with this equipment. It sounds gloomy, but should you become the focus of an air and / or sea rescue search, being in possession of an SMB or similar signalling device, could be the difference between being rescued or lost at sea.

Pony cylinder

> For UK dives deeper than 25 metres I often dive with
> an additional three litre cylinder attached to my 12-litre
cylinder by a clamp – known as a pony. It is comforting to
know that you have a back up plan should your buddy be out
of sight at depth. If you do invest in or perhaps hire a pony,
it is important to adjust your weight accordingly. I usually
shed a couple of kilos if diving with mine, although this will
differ from person to person. The cylinder is often fixed to
one side of your main tank, meaning you will need to shift
some weight to the opposite side to even its distribution.
A buoyancy check will determine whether you are properly
weighted or not.

Ensure that you can reach the tank's valve and of course its regulator when setting the cylinder up. I never use my pony cylinder to extend my dive time, however it is worth practicing its use on a safety stop at the end of your dive, or perhaps in shallow water.

If you tend to guzzle your air quickly (like many new to diving do), it may be worth hiring or purchasing a 15-litre. I often hire a 15-litre cylinder when making a 30 metre dive or deeper.

Accessories

Other than the obvious pieces of kit, (BCD, fins, mask, regulator and cylinder), the following accessories will also aid the UK diver. Some of these items can be obtained cheaply second hand, while others will warrant more of an investment, such as a good torch. Consider back up items of kit too, which may save a dive while at sea, should something break or be lost overboard.

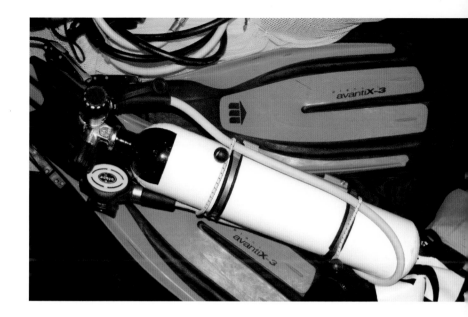

- **Knife or net cutter** The huge Rambo style knives on the market are unnecessary in my opinion, a small BCD knife will be ample.

- **Compass** A handy direction finding device!

- **Torch** Invest in a decent one – light levels vary in UK waters and it could be used as a signalling device at night too.

- **Spare fin straps** If you snap one and nobody has a spare on the boat – it maybe dive over for you.

- **Net bag** Keep your kit together on the dive boat – it can get crowded during the summer months. Handy for lifting a few scallops for tea too!

- **Waterproof boat bag / dry bag** They keep your stuff dry!

- **Second pair of gloves** If making multiple dives in a day, especially in winter months, warm dry gloves for your second dive are a luxury.

- **Compact disc** I keep an old CD in my BCD pocket – an emergency, reflective signalling device.

Cylinders

 Hard boats will often offer two dive packages without returning to shore, meaning that two cylinders will be required for the day. Consider this when booking a trip – do you need to hire or purchase two?

Weather

High winds will often lead to dive centres cancelling boat diving trips. Consider a sheltered shore dive or inland site should this be the case. Wind direction will also have a bearing on a trip being "blown out" or not. Contact the dive centre or boat operator the day before for confirmation. However some boat skippers are bolder than others! The previous week's weather conditions may also have a bearing on the visibility. Again, confirm the conditions with your chosen dive centre prior to the trip.

Tides

Neap tides are especially weak tides and often produce the best visibility. Many divers will plan trips around these tides in order to maximise their enjoyment. Spring tides can have the opposite effect, being the highest of the high tides.

Sun protection

↘ An obvious one perhaps, but you are more likely to
burn or suffer the sun's effects being at or by the sea
all day. Sun block is vital.

Hydration

↘ Keep a bottle of water with you on the dive boat
and drink plenty before and after diving. Breathing
compressed air can be thirsty work. Dehydration can
contribute to decompression sickness in some cases.

Your Limits

 Know your limits. A 30 metre dive in the Red Sea may not seem as challenging as a 30 metre UK dive. Build your experience over several dives. I believe some of the best UK dives are within just 15 metres of water.

CORNWALL

Cornwall is a great county for both boat and shore diving. With access to Porthkerris (the areas most famous shore diving spot), Lizard Point, the Manacles and dozens of interesting coves and beaches, the UK diver is spoilt for choice here. Being surrounded on three sides by the sea, means that divers can usually get wet whatever the weather. Accommodation is in abundance too, from camping and caravan sites, to B&B's and hotels, you will never be stuck for a place to stay. As well as the diving, the scenery topside is of course second to none, meaning you will need a week or several visits to fit it all in!

DRAWNA ROCKS

ACCESS	SHORE
DIVE CENTRE	porthkerris.com
DIVE TYPE	SHORE
DEPTH RANGE	SHORELINE TO 20 METRES

Drawna Rocks (or Dragon Rocks translated from Cornish) is considered to be one of the best shore dives in the country. Located just a few yards out from Porthkerris Divers own beach, you will require several dives to take it all in. It is well protected within the cove and possible to dive at any state of the tide. The site consists of a series of rocky outcrops breaking the surface, clad in kelp just below and bejewelled with jewel anemones deeper still. Sea cucumbers litter the area, with sponges and dead men's fingers feeding in the current. The cuckoo wrasse here are particularly friendly and cannot help but admire themselves vainly in your camera lens or mask. A maze of gullies and cracks make up the site, inhabited by a whole host of critters. Despite being a shore dive, decent depth can be achieved with 20 metres or so possible in parts. John Dory, cuttlefish and occasionally red gurnard can be found here, so keep your eyes peeled. If you would like some help orientating yourself, the dive centre offer guided dives – for a fee. With Porthkerris as your base, it is easy to spend a whole day diving Drawna Rocks, with its well stocked shop, snack wagon and on site air fills, you have no excuse not to!

ACCESS   BOAT
DIVE CENTRE   porthkerris.com
DIVE TYPE   WRECK
DEPTH RANGE   20 METRES

Porthkerris Divers run boats to this wreck site and we dived it from their smaller boat "Celtic Kitten" while on a camping trip to the area. The weather that weekend was perfect, however the huge spring tides meant the visibility was not as good as it could have been. We still enjoyed eight or so metres of viz, but were told it can be twice that. "The Volnay", just five or ten minutes boat ride from Porthkerris, struck a mine in 1917 while on her way back from Canada and loaded with luxury goods and munitions. She is pretty flat now, lying on a silty seabed and in around 20 metres of water (depending on the tide of course). All the brass shells have been salvaged by the wreck's owner and there is no trace of any of the luxury goods which apparently washed ashore shortly after her sinking – lucky locals. It is an easy site to navigate and 45 minutes will be plenty to take much of it in. The highlight for me was the discovery of a garden of pink sea fans covering a vast area. Starfish and urchins are scattered about the place with shoals of bib hiding among broken metal plates and wreckage. We found a long pipe structure poking three metres out of the seabed with every inch encrusted with plumose anemone and dead men's fingers. From here we sent up an SMB and made for the surface after our safety stop. Moments later we were back at Porthkerris Cove chilling out on the beach.

ACCESS	BOAT
DIVE CENTRE	porthkerris.com
DIVE TYPE	WRECK
DEPTH RANGE	15 - 30 METRES

106 lives were lost when the Mohegan (previously the Cleopatra) broke her rudder on Vase Reef and crashed helplessly into rocks know as "The Voices" in 1898. A simple cross marks the mass burial site at nearby village St Keverne. Again, the wreck is just a short boat ride from Porthkerris cove and this time aboard their largest vessel "Celtic Cat". On arrival and after an interesting brief, the skipper will put a shot line in for you to descend and take a look for yourself. The wreck covers a vast area and depths from 15 to nearly 30 metres, so may require several dives to take her all in. As soon as the wreck appears, a tangle of growth covered metal drops away into the depths over a big enough area to accommodate a boat full of divers. This time we decided to explore just the shallower bow section before making our way west to the towering rocky cracks and gullies that make up The Voices. Here we discovered a forest of kelp blowing too and fro in the swell and wall upon wall of jewel anemone lighting up brilliantly under the camera strobe. Huge solitary pollack can be found sheltering among the weedy areas and urchins as big as your head cling to the rock. Combining two dives sites for me is always a bonus, offering additional interest and adding value for money too!

THE CARMARTHEN

ACCESS	BOAT
DIVE CENTRE	porthkerris.com
DIVE TYPE	WRECK
DEPTH RANGE	22 METRES

The Carmarthen is situated west of Porthkerris Dive Centre, further along the coast towards Lizard Point. The 20 minute leisurely boat ride affords stunning views of the Cornish cliffs, its hidden coves and beautiful bays. Torpedoed by German sub UC-50 in 1917, the Carmarthen now rests in around 22 metres of water on a sandy seabed. She did not sink immediately and an attempt was made to beach her before she did. Today, the only recognisable remains are her two huge boilers sitting side by side and conveniently, when we dived her, right by the shot line. She is now well broken up with wreckage standing two to three metres proud of the seabed in parts. Sea fans, sponges and various fish species will keep your interest and combined with good visibility this is a splendid place to hone your camera skills. After 30 minutes of bottom time spent rummaging about the site we made for the surface and were back aboard the Celtic Cat tucking into complimentary tea and sandwiches. The Cat boasts a double diver lift meaning all those diving are brought back aboard with minimal fuss and effort.

THE HELFORD RIVER

ACCESS	BOAT
DIVE CENTRE	porthkerris.com
DIVE TYPE	DRIFT/RIVER
DEPTH RANGE	7 METRES

This is something of a novelty dive, full of life and very relaxing being in just seven metres of water with a gentle current. The Celtic Cat dropped us in just up from the river mouth, where it meets the sea. The river mouth is very wide so feels more like an open water dive than anything else. The informative dive brief detailed possible sightings of thorn backed rays, sea hares, John Dory, cuttlefish and scallops aplenty, so we were eager to get going. We hopped off the boat in the middle of the river and descended to just above the sandy bottom. Empty razor clam shells were strewn everywhere with sprigs of different weed species tumbling about in the current and mid water. Amongst the weed, angry looking spider crabs waved their claws at us in protest as we drifted by. I was on the look out for the photogenic thorn backed ray and after 20 minutes spotted one lying lazily in the sand. The current is gentle enough to allow you to stop and admire whichever creatures you chance upon and then drift to the next once you have had your fill. Scallops are plentiful and can be easily identified poking out of the sand. Due to its shallow nature, an hour is achievable underwater, however if you are in a wet suit, 45 minutes might be more realistic. It is important to remember that you are diving in the middle of a busy river with boat traffic, so your ascent should be made with caution and most definitely on an SMB. Once at the surface, keep an eye on the boat traffic until collected by the dive boat. If you take scallops, the skipper will grade your catch and throw back any considered too small.

ACCESS	BOAT	
DIVE CENTRE	cornishfishing.co.uk	
DIVE TYPE	REEF	
DEPTH RANGE	18 METRES	

We dived this site from an excellent boat named MV Wave Chieftain run by friendly skipper Nigel Hodge. The spacious 42ft x 17ft vessel got us out to the site in 20 minutes, a mile or so off shore. This site consists of a vast rocky reef crawling with starfish, sea cucumbers and urchins. Being early spring meant that the fish life was sparse but the visibility great. Crabs and other crustaceans can be found here hiding among the jagged rocks that cover the area. A constant depth of 18 metres makes this an easy and relaxing dive from start to finish. Aboard Wave Chieftain, post dive, you will be helped back to your seat and furnished with a hot drink and sausage bap – not bad service at all we thought.

Our group spent this weekend camping near Falmouth and the Yacht Club from where we met the boat, was situated only a few miles drive from the campsite.

DEVON

Both the north and south coasts of Devon offer fantastic diving opportunities. The north coast, washed by the Atlantic, can produce fantastic visibility and marine life not often found around the rest of the UK's shores. Seals, porpoises, occasional basking sharks, colourful fans and jellyfish make up a fraction of what Devon's north coast has to offer. The south coast boasts some of the best wreck dives in the country with several well established dive centres servicing them.

LUNDY ISLAND

Lundy Island dive sites north Devon

Lundy Island, managed by The Landmark Trust is a protected marine reserve and a place of great natural beauty. Three miles long and half a mile wide it is situated on the fringes of the Bristol Channel and washed by the cool clear waters of the Atlantic. It is a Mecca for UK divers and as well as an abundance of extraordinary crustaceans, anemones, squirts, jellies and a plethora of fish species to be discovered, it is famous for its seal encounters too. Some of Lundy's shallower shoreline sites make for superb snorkelling spots as well, meaning that non-divers can also take part in the action. There are also a handful of decent wrecks surrounding the island to poke around on for good measure.

↘ It is possible to camp on the island itself or book accommodation in one of its many fascinating buildings which, to mention just a few, include "The Castle", "The Old School" and "Square Cottage". Day trips are possible by purchasing a ticket to board MS Oldenburg, although this route will limit your diving to only one or two restricted spots accessible only from the shore. The best way to get the most out of Lundy's diving is to either stay on the Island and then arrange for a dive boat to collect you each morning, or book a space on one of the hard boats operating from the mainland. There are plenty of campsites and B&B's in and around Ilfracombe, from where dive boat operators will collect divers each morning. Typically dive boats leave for Lundy at 8am, returning around 4pm

THE KNOLL PINS

i		
ACCESS	BOAT	
DIVE CENTRE	obsessionboatcharters.co.uk,	
	clovelly-charters.ukf.net	
DIVE TYPE	PINNACLE	
DEPTH RANGE	8 - 20 METRES	

Often the first dive of the day at Lundy, the "Knoll Pins" are a pair of submerged rocky pinnacles situated a couple of hundred metres from the islands cliffs. The first thing you will notice when you descend is the (usually) fantastic visibility and unique variety of marine life, you could be forgiven for thinking you were diving abroad. It is possible to navigate the Pins in a figure of eight starting near the sandy seabed at around 17 metres, slowly working your way shallower as you wind your way round. The kelp clad Pins are home to an abundance of sea urchins, sea cucumbers, fans, soft corals, jelly and starfish. Also waiting to be discovered on one side is a gorge like rock formation, where there is enough space to swim through. Care should be taken not to damage this site, as its walls are littered on either side with delicate pink sea fans – be careful where you put those fins. As a protected reserve, Lundy is therefore a "no-take" zone, so you will have to leave your goody bag aboard the boat. After sending up your SMB, a safety stop will be carried out somewhere near the top of the Pins and once back aboard the boat, you will be welcomed with a cup of tea or fresh mackerel if you are with the right skipper!

i

ACCESS	BOAT
DIVE CENTRE	obsessionboatcharters.co.uk,
	clovelly-charters.ukf.net
DIVE TYPE	BAY - SHALLOW SEAL ENCOUNTER
DEPTH RANGE	5 - 10 METRES

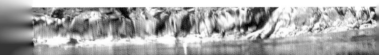

Seal Encounter!

Looking back at my logbook for this dive, it appears I have written simply "seal madness!" The purpose of this dive is therefore to encounter at close quarters, Lundy's resident grey seals or "halichoerus grypus", which translates as "hook-nosed pig". It is said that up to 120 seals inhabit the island's rocky ledges (depending on the time of year) and when you visit the island, it is easy to see why this spot suits them perfectly. Divers are usually dropped in by boat around 40 metres or so away from the rocky shoreline, from where you will descend to around ten metres before making your way into much shallower water. Alternatively you can easily surface swim to the shoreline. At around four to five metres, the seabed becomes rocky and kelp covered, where the inquisitive grey seals will soon appear. The anticipation of this extraordinary encounter adds real excitement to the dive experience and when the creatures show up, they will put on a real display. The seals seem to be most attracted to brightly coloured fins and hoses and will playfully nibble on gloves and exposure suits. While seemingly clumsy and awkward on land, these almost dog-like creatures are quick and agile underwater, darting too and fro at considerable speed. They are also very photogenic, so make sure you take your camera to record this fabulous encounter. The seals come and go throughout the dive at Gannet's and during their absence it is worth exploring closer to the rocky shoreline, poking about in the weedy gullies and overhangs that make it up. In just four or five metres of water the visibility and light here is often excellent and with the playful seals added to the equation, this spot makes for a most memorable dive.

ACCESS	BOAT
DIVE CENTRE	obsessionboatcharters.co.uk,
	clovelly-charters.ukf.net
DIVE TYPE	WRECK
DEPTH RANGE	18 - 25 METRES

The "MV Robert" – a cargo ship that came to grief in 1976, is just one of the many diveable wrecks that litter Lundy's shores. She is around 50 metres in length and lies on her starboard side pretty much intact in about 25 metres of water. Her port side rises to 18 metres below the surface, making for an interesting multilevel dive with something for all abilities. The usually super visibility means that a decent proportion of this wreck can be photographed using a wide-angle lens and there is always plenty for the macro photographer. There is no shortage of nooks and crannies to poke around in with your torch and the giant resident lobster can be found at the seabed, minding its own business. The wreck is colourfully decorated with plumose anemones, sponges, dead men's fingers, and pollack and wrasse can be found carpeting or hanging about the Robert. A couple of grumpy looking conger eels reside there too, so watch where you put those fingers. The wreck is easily navigable and can be fully explored in one dive finishing back at the mooring line. Several species of jellyfish fill the water column during your ascent, and make for great subjects to photograph or observe while passing the time on your safety stop.

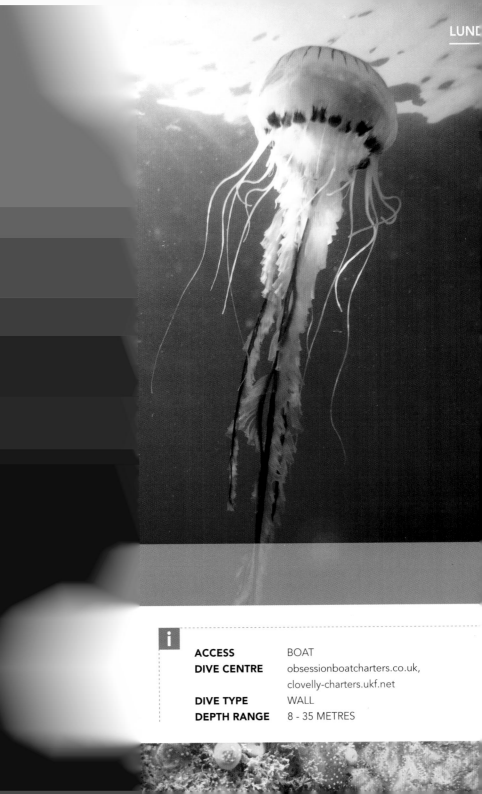

ACCESS	BOAT
DIVE CENTRE	obsessionboatcharters.co.uk,
	clovelly-charters.ukf.net
DIVE TYPE	WALL
DEPTH RANGE	8 - 35 METRES

We dived this site, just around the corner from Gannet's Bay, while on a combined camping / diving trip to Lundy Island. Our group chartered friendly and knowledgeable skipper Clive Pearson's boat "Jessica Hettie" for the weekend. When slack water finally came and once we had finished our lunch of fresh mackerel (caught that day outside of the no-take zone of course), Clive dropped us in 30 odd metres from the rock itself where we descended eight or so metres to the top of the wall. The visibility was so good that you could clearly see the kelp covered wall top from the boat's bow. The top and southern side of the wall are mainly covered with kelp and weed, sloping gently to a sandy sea floor at around 13 metres. If you fin along this side of the wall, after a few minutes it can become a little repetitive. Navigate the site properly and you will find yourself enjoying a colourful display for yard upon yard of jewel anemones of every colour imaginable. This site is a playground for the macro photographer with little to no current on the right tide and super visibility. Follow the wall to the northwest and you will finally reach Lundy's cliffs, where in three or four metres of water, you might chance upon a few seals.

CARMINE FILOMENA

ACCESS	BOAT
DIVE CENTRE	obsessionboatcharters.co.uk, clovelly-charters.ukf.net
DIVE TYPE	WRECK
DEPTH RANGE	8 - 15 METRES

This shallow wreck is situated close to the rocks of "Rat Island" and a short boat ride from Lundy's jetty. She was an Italian steam powered cargo vessel and sank after running aground in 1937. Her remains cover a fairly large area with the only identifiable parts being the propeller shaft, some steel ribs and part of the remaining hull. The bow is situated by the rocks of Rat Island, in around eight metres of water with the stern section deeper in 15 metres. Most of the wreckage is covered with kelp producing nooks and crannies to explore and home to spider crabs and occasionally cuttlefish or their egg sacks. Sizeable wrasse and starfish also make this wreck their home with some big pollack dotted about for good measure. The Carmine was carrying coal when she sank and the odd rounded lump can still be seen rolling about on the sandy seabed. A permanent shot line is attached to part of the steel remains making entry and exit easy – if you can find it again at the end of the dive of course. Failing that, ascending on an SMB will allow the boat to pick you up safely. Care should be taken to avoid venturing too far round the southern part of Rat Island, as strong currents can be present here. Again, we dived this wreck from Clive Pearson's boat "Jessica Hettie" (Clovelly Charters).

ACCESS	BOAT
DIVE CENTRE	aquanauts.co.uk
DIVE TYPE	WRECK
DEPTH RANGE	18 - 26 METERS

South Devon

Ok, so technically the wreck of HMS Scylla is in Cornwall, however on this occasion we dived her from Plymouth, with established dive centre "Aquanauts". She was sunk in 2004 in Whitsand Bay as an artificial reef and as the years have ticked by, her portfolio of marine residents has increased. She sits just 25 minutes boat ride from Plymouth. The wreck used to be marked with floating steel drums attached to it by chains. The drums have over the years broken away, meaning that boat skippers have to locate the wreck and put a shot onto it for divers to descend. Visibility wise, you can expect anything from a hideous one metre to a glorious 20, so pretty varied. On the occasion we dived the Scylla, we were met with an average to gloomy three metres. With hindsight, I would have perhaps called the dive centre and established the optimum time to dive to enjoy the best viz. This is an enormous wreck and due to its age, is still very much in one piece, so it goes with out saying that you will want to be impressed by its gargantuan size in good viz. Deck level can be found at an easy 18 metres with every surface home to plumose anemones and dead men's fingers. Shoals of small pollack can be seen using overhangs and metal structures as shelter. Drop deeper still, follow the side of the hull and you will be met with several huge holes offering entry to the wreck. Owing to the poor viz when we made the dive, we chose not to go in, but understand that penetration can be made easily. It goes without saying that one should enter at their own risk and perhaps do so with a diver who has experience of the site's interior. We found the wreck's bow and followed the port side in a gentle current just below the railings, before sending up an SMB and then picked up by the boat 40 minutes later. HMS Scylla is a well known and popular wreck and due to her size will definitely require several visits.

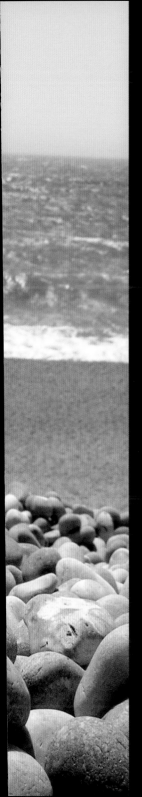

DORSET

You will need all your fingers and toes to count the dives sites accessible from Dorset's shores. It is also home to some of the finest beaches on the south coast and mile upon mile of stunning scenery. Dorset's coastline is strewn with wreckage from both world wars, victims of fog and foundered cargo vessels, all producing exciting exploration for the wreck enthusiast. Exciting drift dives and vast reefs also attract divers of all levels. Portland is perhaps one of the most popular destinations for the UK diver, while Swanage is a favourite spot for the novice diver, combining both shore and boat diving from one handy base. I believe that these are two of the most accessible places on the south coast to take the plunge and discover UK diving.

PORTLAND

The Isle of Portland

Well placed for UK divers of all levels, Portland is one of a few destinations where you will usually be able to dive whatever the weather. Its huge harbour, located on the east side of the Isle of Portland is one of the largest man made harbours in the world, and when most dives are blown out along the coast, the wrecks inside the harbour walls are almost always accessible by boat. The harbour wall or "breakwater" also offers the chance to enjoy gentle drift dives along it at 18 metres where you will discover a plethora of marine life. Portland offers the chance to explore a variety of sites and with so many to choose from, you will need several visits to explore them all.

Certain sites will only be suitable to dive at slack water, which means the boat will need to leave on time in order to make this potentially narrow window. It is a good idea to turn up at the dive centre at least an hour before the boat leaves for the dive.

THE
COUNTESS OF ERNE

ACCESS	BOAT FROM WEYMOUTH OR PORTLAND
DIVE CENTRE	fathomandblues.co.uk, scimitardiving.co.uk
DIVE TYPE	WRECK
DEPTH RANGE	10 - 15 METRES

The Countess of Erne, 80 metres in length was originally a paddle steamer and in later life a coal hulk. She sank in 1935 after her moorings broke loose. The wreck today sits recognisably upright in 15 metres of water and is located only a few yards from the harbour wall. The deck section sits at around eight metres from the surface, making for a popular local dive. Its accessibility means that the site can become busy in peak season, although its size means that groups can spread out, so you should only bump into one or two fellow wreckies on your way. A permanent mooring is attached to at least one end of the Countess, where you will be dropped over the wreck in small groups or buddy pairs. Once you have descended onto the wreck, a lap of her hull is recommended, where you will inevitably meet her giant rudder - an excellent wide-angle photo opportunity if visibility is on your side. The Countess is penetrable in parts, however owing to the silty nature of the seabed, the visibility can quickly disappear. I would only recommend a tour inside with an experienced companion and of course competent buoyancy. This site is a favourite with wreck training courses.

Once you have completed the lap, it is time to explore the deck area, where you will find plenty of cuckoo and ballan wrasse, rock cooks and sponges. We have even spotted squat lobster and lump suckers here too. Air permitting you should have plenty of time left for bimbling around this area, finishing the dive on the mooring line where the boat will pick you up.

GROVE POINT

ℹ️

ACCESS	BOAT
DIVE CENTRE	fathomandblues.co.uk, scimitardiving.co.uk
DIVE TYPE	DRIFT
DEPTH RANGE	20 METRES +

Grove point is situated on the east side of Portland, past Balaclava Bay and before Church Ope Bay. Local dive centres regularly run RIB's and hard boats to this area and the dive site is classified as a "drift". The depth varies here, so dives can be made any where from 20 metres and beyond, it can be hit and miss as to where the boat will put you, however the skipper will usually ask his divers what depth they are happy with before dropping you in. I have dived this site on several occasions, usually landing at around the 25-metre mark, although you can find yourself going much deeper quite quickly in the current so care should be taken to watch your depth. The boat's skipper will require his divers to deploy an SMB on reaching the bottom, which can be a challenging task to carry out in a fast current once at the sea bed. For ease, you can always inflate your buoy at the surface and descend deploying line from your reel. Once the buoy is up and you and your fellow divers are settled, hold on, as this drift can be exhilarating! Scallops can often be found at Grove Point too, so take a torch to make spotting them easier. It is possible you will encounter the odd dogfish and you will certainly bump into spider and edible crabs. Depending on your air consumption, gas mix and exposure suit, you will probably get 40 minutes out of this dive. Grove Point is a splendid dive, quick and easy to get to by boat and if the sun is shining you will enjoy the scenery too and from the dive site as well.

LULWORTH BANKS

ACCESS	BOAT FROM WEYMOUTH OR PORTLAND
DIVE CENTRE	fathomandblues.co.uk, scimitardiving.co.u
DIVE TYPE	DRIFT/REEF
DEPTH RANGE	10 - 22 METRES

The stunning scenery en route to the site is one of the reasons to actually go and experience this dive. You feel like you are getting your money's worth if you actually enjoy the boat ride as well as the dive. The impressive Dorset cliffs and Durdle Door on a sunny day, make the boat trip out to the banks a more than pleasurable experience. The site or "banks" themselves vary in depth depending on where you are dropped and can range from around 10 – 22 or so metres in depth. The seabed can vary visually too, from sandy barren patches with not a huge amount going on, to a rocky reef system with drop offs and rugged underwater scenery. These rugged areas are often teeming with life and some divers go specifically to collect scallops. A super and varied dive site with something different to see on each visit.

LANDING CRAFT & BOMBARDON UNIT

ACCESS	BOAT FROM WEYMOUTH OR PORTLAND
DIVE CENTRE	fathomandblues.co.uk, scimitardiving.co.u
DIVE TYPE	WRECK
DEPTH RANGE	7 - 16 METRES

These two sites are situated in close proximity to one another, hence listing them together. They are situated at the same end of Portland harbour as the Countess of Erne and both can be explored in one dive. A rope links one to the other conveniently. The permanent shot line can be found at the bow of this WW2 landing craft, and because of the wreck's simplicity, will not take you long to explore. It is around ten metres in length, fairly intact and quite an interesting wreck, however the marine life surrounding it can be sparse. It is worth poking around nearer the seabed and around the diesel engines at the stern with your torch, but nothing much appears to live within the intact deck area itself. A rope connecting this site to the Bombardon unit can be found at the stern behind the wheelhouse and after following this for a few minutes (depending on how hard you fin) brings you to part two of the dive.

The Bombardon Unit, invented as a temporary pontoon and wave breaking system in WW2, makes for a reasonably interesting dive. It is around 50 metres in length with the top section at seven metres from the surface, depending on the tide. Its interesting structure allows you to peer inside with the torch and parts of it are penetrable, although I personally would not want to enter it. There are plenty of fish about, as well as the odd crab here and there. A length along the east side of the wreck and back over the top will be as much as you will want to do, before making your way back to the shot on the Landing Craft. If you do surface away from the line, swim away from the harbour wall, as the boat will not want to manoeuvre too close to it when picking divers up.

THE M2 SUBMARINE

ACCESS BOAT FROM WEYMOUTH OR PORTLAND

DIVE CENTRE fathomandblues.co.uk, scimitardiving.co.u

DIVE TYPE WRECK

DEPTH RANGE 28 - 35 METRES

An intact 296ft submarine sitting upright in 35 metres of water, the M2 is an exciting wreck to dive. She tragically sank in January 1932 with the loss of all her crew. The vessel was equipped with a small sea going biplane with folding wings and a fault with its hanger doors led to her demise. Local dive centres run trips to the M2 when conditions and tides are right but I would only advise booking a space if furnished with some deep UK diving experience. The wreck is found a couple of miles off shore on the west side of Chesil Beach, so it means with dive boats launching from the east side of Portland harbour, the journey can take 40 minutes. The position of the dive site allows you to take in all of Portland's fabulous coast line on the way, however you may want to consider booking a place on a local hard boat for added comfort. Once over the dive site, the skipper will drop a shot line over board in order to allow the group to descend it onto the wreck. Once you have kitted up, completed your buddy checks and descended the shot, the impressive Sub will appear at around 28 metres. Navigation of the wreck is easy, with your only options being stern to bow and back (or vice versa depending on where the shot has put you). You can either follow the line all the way to the seabed (take a good torch) and explore the underside of the wreck, or stay at deck or "pressure hull" level increasing your bottom time. The conning tower (rising some nine or so metres off the pressure hull) and hanger are clearly identifiable with the hanger (always teaming with fish) being the penetrable part. I would avoid entering the any part of the M2, as it is full of silt inside, so you are better off viewing the interior peering in with your torch. The wreck is a haven for all manner of marine life from conger eels, cod, crustaceans and starfish, to brightly coloured sponges and dead men's fingers. The visibility can vary from a challenging two or three metres to a glorious ten plus. The M2 is a spectacular dive site so worth taking a camera and many UK divers will want it featuring in their logbook.

ACCESS		BOAT FROM WEYMOUTH OR PORTLANI
DIVE CENTRE		fathomandblues.co.uk, scimitardiving.co.ui
DIVE TYPE		WRECK & HARBOUR WALL
DEPTH RANGE		10 METRES

Not a huge amount is known about the Dredger or how it came to be where it is in Balaclava Bay. It is a very easy dive accessible by boat, sitting in only ten metres of water just outside the harbour wall. It is well broken up consisting of metal plates and steel remains jutting out from the sandy bottom in every direction. Fish life is plentiful for such a shallow and simple wreck, with decent shoals of bib and pollack taking refuge in every nook and cranny.

The site will not take you long to explore, so I would recommend heading in a northerly direction towards the harbour wall in order to add interest to the dive. Take a torch, as the boulders that make up the harbour wall are quite big, creating a cave like habitat for all manner of critters. This dive is perfect for the novice diver and due to the lack of current here and its shallow proximity, means visibility is usually quite good.

ACCESS	SHORE	
DIVE CENTRE	fathomandblues.co.uk	
DIVE TYPE	SHORE	
DEPTH RANGE	SHORE TO 18 METRES	

Chesil Cove is an excellent shore dive with easy access by the Cove House Inn. There are three car parks to choose from so establishing a base for the day should not be a problem. The beach is situated on the right hand side of Portland, at the end of the Chesil Beach road. This area is sheltered from easterly winds by Portland's cliffs, but can be choppy and best avoided with a westerly blowing. Air fills and kit hire can be obtained from a number of local centres. Once submerged, the seabed drops off forming a series of shelves and eventually becoming rocky in places. Explore further out and the seabed becomes sandy. The dive site is full of life all year round with a variety of wrasse, common pipefish, tom pot blennies and the odd John Dory hovering here and there. The sandy patches are home to schools of sand eels, lobster and edible crabs hiding among the bigger rocks. Sea bass and pollack can often be spotted, with cuttlefish present in the spring and early summer. Local dive centres offer escorted dives here too, although it is essential to check weather conditions before planning a trip to Chesil. The Cove House Inn is a great spot for a post dive bite to eat and pint of local ale.

Swanage dive sites

 As well as the superb diving, Swanage makes for a
fantastic holiday or long weekend offering something
to suit all diving enthusiasts. There are plenty of campsites,
B&B's and good pubs in the area and the quaint town is
popular in summer with holidaymakers. Divers gather on the
pier making it their base for shore diving under the pier and
surrounding area and using the pontoon and pier itself to

board boats for local wreck, reef and drift dives. Post dive, it is worth driving to Corfe Castle just a few miles outside Swanage for lunch in one of the pubs or an exploration of the ruins themselves.

ACCESS	SHORE OR FROM THE PIER ITSELF
DIVE CENTRE	diversdownswanage.co.uk
DIVE TYPE	SHORE
DEPTH RANGE	4 - 5 METRES

Swanage Pier is a great starting point for those wishing to "discover UK diving". Easy access means that novice divers can hone their skills and become accustom to UK waters in relative safety. Conveniently, there is a well-stocked shop and dive centre on the pier (Divers Down) providing air fills and essential kit. The owners also run two dive boats (more on those later). There is also a teashop close by and the popular traditional seaside town is only yards away from the pier.

Although the pier can be dived at any time, you will make more of the limited depth if dived at high tide. Resident marine life includes plenty of ballan wrasse, blennies, anemone, and crabs. Be careful when you reach the far end of the pier, as this area is popular with fishermen and a fair amount of line can be found in the water – not always attached to the end of a rod. Dive boats come and go from the left hand side of the pier too, so watch out for their propellers. Move away from the pier, to the right and you may chance upon the odd pipefish. They are very well camouflaged so a keen eye will be required to spot one hiding among the grassy patches. The seabed here is sandy and the visibility often excellent as a result.

Adjacent to the Victorian pier you will notice the remains of the "old pier"; this part is directly accessible from Divers Down's pontoon, behind the shop (seek permission from the shop to use this first). It is a brighter dive, as none of its decking remains, however this site can be busy with boat traffic so caution should be taken when on or near the surface. The area is quite weedy, making an ideal home for a variety of species. Losing your bearings is surprisingly easy owing to the curved shape of the pier's remaining posts. However it is shallow, so easy to surface and regroup if you do. Both piers are good spots to sharpen your camera, buoyancy or SMB deployment skills and the visibility is usually good.

PEVERIL LEDGES

ACCESS	BOAT FROM SWANAGE
DIVE CENTRE	diversdownswanage.co.uk
DIVE TYPE	DRIFT
DEPTH RANGE	13 - 25 METRES

If it is a flying experience you are after, this is the site for you. Dropping down through the water column the seabed suddenly appears at 13 metres, whizzing by beneath you at a cracking pace. We dived Peveril Ledges on a neap tide, the lowest of the high tides occurring twice a month. Neaps often produce super visibility and on this occasion it did just that. After a few minutes of passing over flat, reasonably featureless seabed (except for a dog fish and several crabs), the ledges suddenly came at us. They are almost ramp-like in their appearance and often two or more metres of depth can be lost as you "take off". A quick glance back once over the top reveals a bank of sand and fine shingle with crabs and fish sheltering from the current. As well as looking down, look forward too to save the embarrassment of crashing into rocks at speed. Before reaching the next one the drift can slow down somewhat as the current decides which direction it is heading. We agreed on a maximum depth before making the dive, as it can drop to 25 metres in the gullies between the ledges. If you decide to stop at 20 metres or shallower as we did, you will find the seabed can disappear from sight at times, don't fret; it will be back in view just moments later. Owing to the yoyo effect the seabed creates, you will find yourself adjusting your buoyancy more often than you might usually, it is part and parcel of this dive site so go with it. Surfacing, we were met again by Divers Down boat "Swanage Diver", scooped up by its diver lift and sipping hot chocolates by the stunning cliffs moments later. While enjoying our hot drinks we admired a flock of shags basking in the afternoon sun, apparently perching on their favourite spot "shit rock" – much to our amusement. A cracking drift dive and well worth repeating.

ACCESS   BOAT FROM SWANAGE
DIVE CENTRE   diversdownswanage.co.uk
DIVE TYPE   WRECK & DRIFT COMBINED
DEPTH RANGE   14 METRES

 The "Fleur de Lys" was a fishing trawler that apparently sank relatively recently whilst on tow to Poole. "Divers Down" operates spacious hard boats that will take you to this wreck only five minutes ride from their pontoon, although unlike Portland dive centres, "Divers Down" boats may only be running during the diving "season". The permanently shot wreck is fairly broken up, although parts of the wooden hull are still recognisable. Sitting upright in 14 metres of water the wreck is home to an abundance of life. Shoals of bib, solitary John Dory and lobster have all colonised the Fleur de Lys. There is often a slight current running over the wreck, which means after 15 minutes or so exploring the Fleur de Lys, you can leave the wreck to enjoy a gentle drift, adding variety to the dive. Your skipper will ask you to send up a buoy once off the wreck in order to keep track of the group. The seabed is reasonably featureless although the marine life is there - keep your eyes peeled and you may stumble across a thorn back ray settled on the sand. Edible and velvet swimming crabs also frequent the area as well as the odd scallop and on a one trip, I encountered an exotic looking sea lemon slug. The dive will take around 45 minutes to complete and once back aboard the boat there will be just enough time for a complimentary hot chocolate before arriving back in Swanage.

HAMPSHIRE

Many of the dive sites I have featured here are accessible from the Portsmouth area, with some dive centres and boat operators visiting some of the sites I have also detailed in the West Sussex section of this book - especially Witterings and Selsey which are only a few miles east along the coast. With the Isle of Wight on its doorstep, Portsmouth is a superb place to catch a boat from and dive local Isle of Wight sites and indeed some of the popular wrecks situated in more exposed areas. It is possible to dive some of the forts and old wartime defence structures here, with Portsmouth being an important naval city during the world's wars as well as today. There are many dive centres operating in and around the Portsmouth area, I have featured a handfull I know of to get you started.

THE CAMBERWELL

ℹ️

ACCESS	BOAT
DIVE CENTRE	wightdiver.co.uk, tritonscuba.co.uk
DIVE TYPE	WRECK
DEPTH RANGE	30 METRES

The Camberwell is a wreck I will never tire of diving. Situated on the eastern side of the Isle of Wight (Sandown Bay) and lying in 30 metres of water makes for a relatively deep dive with obvious bottom time and breathing gas considerations. The spacious hard boat "Wight Diver" ferried us here from the Hayling ferry pontoon at Eastney and the boat ride itself took just over an hour, which is fine if the sun is shining of course! This WW1 cargo steamer is to this day still covered with the remains of her wares. Bottles and jars of all sizes, shapes and colours litter the seabed and wreckage, which makes for an interesting rummage. Divers have previously found blocks of prepaid postcards destined for British troops stationed in India. Lobsters and crabs are in abundance here and the visibility on the right tide means you can be spoiled with a clear 15 metres plus. I discovered the vessels huge anchor right by the shot line and the bow and stern sections are relatively intact with amidships section broken up and closer to the seabed. I would strongly recommend a trip to the Camberwell taking a decent size cylinder and nitrox if you can. I dived this wreck on air and could have done with the extra bottom time to keep exploring.

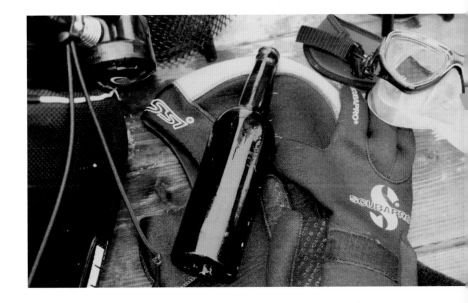

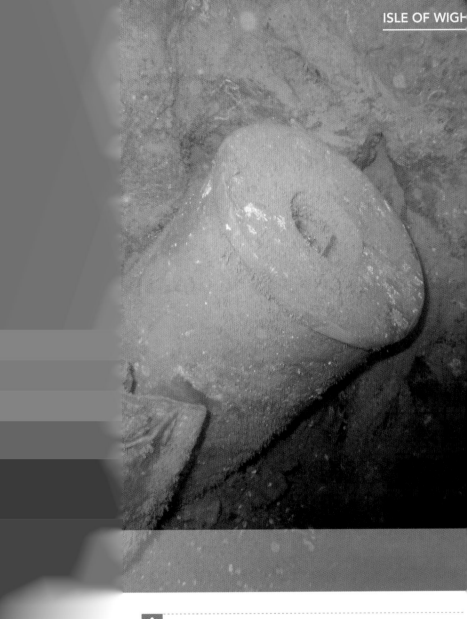

ACCESS	BOAT
DIVE CENTRE	wightdiver.co.uk, tritonscuba.co.uk
DIVE TYPE	WRECK
DEPTH RANGE	12 METRES

Another victim of German torpedo's, the Louis is also situated in Sandown Bay off the Isle of Wight. Again, we hitched a ride on Wight Divers hard boat, making this trip a local second dive after visiting the Camberwell. The main features of this shallow wreck are its two enormous boilers and the remains of its cargo – anti personnel shells strewn about the seabed. Upon reaching the bottom the first thing you will probably notice, apart from the wreck of course are thousands of 12mm diameter ball bearing type objects. These are the deadly contents of the shell casings designed to wreak havoc on the battlefield with anything they connected with. Several crates of intact shells can been seen about the Louis which apart from the boilers make for the main feature of the wreck. It is possible that, and depending when it is dived, this site can double up as a drift dive, taking you further a field and eventually picked up by the boat when you are ready to ascend. The skipper will ask divers to inflate an SMB once on the drift of course. It is well worth visiting this site and makes for a great second dive if spending the day aboard a hard boat. RIB's will visit the area from Triton Scuba too if you would like to get there and back quickly.

ACCESS	GUN WHARF QUAYS - PORTSMOUTH
DIVE CENTRE	adventurecollege.co.uk
DIVE TYPE	CONFINED
DEPTH RANGE	6 METRES

Gunwharf Quays offers a unique blend of outlet shopping, leisure, and entertainment on Portsmouth Harbour, the diving site is right in the middle of the centre. Stocked with marine life by Southsea's Blue Reef Aquarium, this cosy site offers the opportunity to dive in a safe environment, practice skills or develop your diver training in small groups with an instructor. Adventure College, located in Portsmouth, have exclusivity over the diving here so courses or dive sessions should be booked through them directly. The site offers the chance to meet their huge resident lobster, wrasse and grey mullet to mention a few inhabitants. There is also a training platform at five metres, which helps maintain the visibility and from new divers disturbing the silty bottom. Adventure College offer night diving sessions here too, which often draws an audience of bemused shoppers. Gun Wharf Quays is an ideal place to begin your UK diving experience and a chance to familiarise yourself with its challenges before making for the coast.

ACCESS	BOAT
DIVE CENTRE	wightdiver.co.uk, tritonscuba.co.uk
DIVE TYPE	WRECK
DEPTH RANGE	28 METRES

Another casualty of WW1, the Highland Brigade, formerly a Steamship spends her time these days broken up in 28 metres of water on the east side off the Isle of Wight. Again, this is not considered a shallow dive where those "discovering UK diving" are concerned, but certainly one to pop on the list once you have built up your confidence and indeed experience. She is a popular wreck with Portsmouth based dive centres and often the first dive in a two-dive package. The wreck site covers a vast area and much of her cargo of candlestick telephones can still be seen strewn about the sea floor or poking from the twisted remains of the former vessel. The bow still sits upright and its gun is, I am told still in situ, somewhere. Whilst diving this wreck with friends, we chanced upon several items of chinaware buried in the sand and bundles of porcelain electrical insulators, which must have been involved with the telephone equipment still sitting there. The bow section sits upright and five or six meters proud of the sandy seabed. The wreckage forms a number of swim through section in parts; however, remember you are in relatively deep water here so I would only attempt these in great visibility. The hull's ribs are easily identified, offering shelter to a number of fish species and the usual crustacean suspects inhabit the site too. If like me, you like to keep your equipment on the simple side, you will not be spending too long exploring the Highland Brigade owing to bottom time restrictions, however it is not going anywhere, so if you do enjoy your diving here, come back and experience the rest of it another day.

WEST SUSSEX

The local dive centres in and around Witterings and Selsey are both accommodating and helpful and the sites accessible by their boats suit all levels of qualification. Whether you want to explore wartime wrecks, rocky reefs or gentle drift dives collecting prehistoric fossils, this part of the Sussex coast has it all. The Lifeboat Station pier at Selsey also makes for a cracking shallow shore dive.

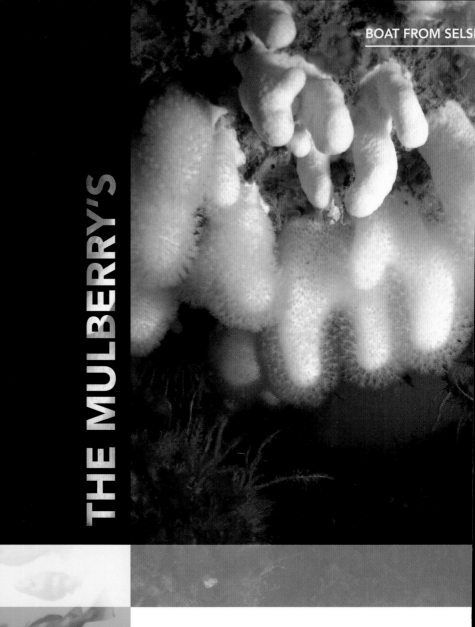

THE MULBERRY'S

i

ACCESS	BOAT
DIVE CENTRE	southerncoastcharters.com, witteringdiver
	mulberrydivers.co.uk, selsey-fish-trips.com
DIVE TYPE	WRECK
DEPTH RANGE	12 METRES

Mulberry Harbours were huge concrete structures built as floating temporary harbours to aid the Normandy landings of 1944. This particular harbour never made France, sinking in 12 metres of water about a mile off shore. This site, in my opinion makes for one of the most interesting dives along the West Sussex coast. A RIB will on average takes 20 minutes to reach the sheltered spot and trips can be booked with a variety of reputable outfits including - Wittering Divers, Southern Coast Boat Charters and Mulberry Divers to mention a few. Visibility is often fantastic and with the mangled concrete and iron remains covering a vast area, it is home to huge shoals of bib, bream, pollack, lobsters, shrimp, blennies and conger eels. This is an easy site to navigate visually and with so much going on, you will want to stay as long as your air allows you to. Be careful where you swim, as some of the exposed reinforcing steel rods have over the decades turned into rusty spikes – you won't want to kebab yourself on one of those. The safety stop, usually completed back on the mooring chain, provides a good opportunity to flick through some of your digital snaps while off gassing. I will never tire of diving The Mulberry's and discover something new each time I do.

LANDING CRAFT

ACCESS	BOAT	
DIVE CENTRE	southerncoastcharters.com, witteringdive	
	mulberrydivers.co.uk, selsey-fish-trips.con	
DIVE TYPE	WRECK	
DEPTH RANGE	8 - 10 METRES	

The remains of this WW2 Landing Craft make for an interesting shallow wreck dive. The wreck sits four metres proud of the seabed with its stern and bow still reasonably intact. In parts the structure provides a swim through, where you will meet most of its residents.

At certain times of year triggerfish can be found here – usually associated with warmer, tropical diving. Small conger can be spotted from time to time, with pouting, whiting and wrasse being more common at the site. As with most UK wrecks, gloves will be essential as the rusty metal plates are sharp in places and won't take much to cut wet hands. We dived the Landing Craft with Wittering Divers (RIB). This is a decent little wreck, with minimum effort involved.

SELSEY LIFEBOAT STATION PIER

ACCESS		SHORE
DIVE CENTRE		witteringdivers.co.uk, mulberrydivers.co.u
DIVE TYPE		SHORE / PIER
DEPTH RANGE		6 METRES

Selsey's Lifeboat Station pier makes for a very easy and pleasurable dive. It is important that the dive is made at the right time though, usually three hours after high water. Dive it at the wrong time and you are in danger of being swept off the site by strong currents – we witnessed two divers making this mistake when we arrived, they made it to shore in one piece but minus a fin. Free street parking and a grassy kitting up area can be found only a short 20 metre walk from the pier on a residential road and there is a tempting looking pub only 100 yards away too - perfect for a post dive refreshment and debrief. Entry to this site is made under the pier itself and once submerged and if the visibility is good, navigation can be made visually by following the pier's legs until you find the lifeboat's launching ramp at the end. Divers are required to tow an inflated SMB at all times in order to make themselves known to the stations crew and you really should avoid hanging around at the end of the ramp, owing to risk to yourself and of course holding up a possible launch. The dive itself is shallow at six metres or so, but much marine life including cuttlefish galore, octopus, sea lemon slugs, anemone and wrasse can be spotted, using the pier as a safe haven. A good hour can be spent enjoying this dive due to its depth and safe environment. This can be a popular site with divers and for good reason, but it is still possible not to bump into one another due to the pier's length. Surfacing is made back at the beach again of course, exit onto the beach is fairly simple and after dumping the kit in your car, that pub may require a visit.

i		
ACCESS	BOAT	
DIVE CENTRE	southerncoastcharters.com, witteringdive	
	mulberrydivers.co.uk, selsey-fish-trips.con	
DIVE TYPE	DRIFT	
DEPTH RANGE	10 - 12 METRES	

A seam of clay runs from the South Downs and into the Sussex coast from which on the sea floor, among other species, fossilised prehistoric ragged tooth, requiem and mackerel shark's teeth can be found. Along side these; fragments of manta ray mandible fossils may also be spotted. Local West Sussex dive centres run trips out to Bracklesham Bay where, if you know what you are looking for, will see a diver discover ten or more fossils in one dive – some of which reach an impressive size. Many local skippers will have a bag of fossilised teeth and mandibles onboard, giving you an idea of how to identify them before you splash in. In parts, some of the clay seam is exposed, forming two metre plus diameter circles in the sandy sea floor, often exposing the densest areas for fossils. Once you have found one, you will soon find others. Take some time to look up from the fossil beds – you may even chance upon the odd cuttlefish hovering about. Several crab species and lobster also make their homes here too, providing enough variety to keep the discerning diver entertained. A superb dive site and one I would dive over and over again.

ACCESS	BOAT
DIVE CENTRE	southerncoastcharters.com, witteringdivers.
	mulberrydivers.co.uk, selsey-fish-trips.com
DIVE TYPE	REEF / DRIFT
DEPTH RANGE	15 METRES

 "The Waldrens" is a cracking dive site combining rocky reef with a gentle drift and at just 15 metres maximum depth, makes for an easy and interesting bimble. The dive site is accessed by boat, in this case Southern Boat Charters' RIB, skippered by Simon Bradburn. Wittering Divers and Mulberry Divers both take divers to this site too. The Waldrens is just five minutes boat ride (RIB) further east of the Mulberry's, so only about 25 minutes boat ride in total. Once we had rolled off the boat and made the short decent, we found the reef to be stacked with life and must have spotted at least six dogfish dozing on the seabed in as many minutes. If you look carefully in the clay / sand seabed you will find the odd shark's tooth fossil or manta ray mandible. The weed covered rocks are home to spider crabs, lobster and all kinds of wrasse including the striking electric blue cuckoo wrasse. A huge shoal of bib at one point followed us too. The site gently slopes down from around ten metres to 15 and it is in the deeper parts you might be lucky enough to pick up one or two scallops. On the occasion we dived this spot we only found two so left them there, but I am told there are plenty about. Look carefully and you will spot the odd cuttlefish and often they will hang about long enough for you to get a really good look or a decent photograph. Being a shallow dive site means you can get a good hours bottom time here and with a good mix of rocks, weed and seabed habitats to explore, means there is enough to keep you interested for the duration. We willl definitely visit the Waldren's again.

ACCESS	BOAT
DIVE CENTRE	southerncoastcharters.com, witteringdive
	mulberrydivers.co.uk, selsey-fish-trips.com
DIVE TYPE	WRECK
DEPTH RANGE	22 METRES

We dived this wreck from a superb hard boat complete with diver lift called "Emma Jayne", owned by experienced and friendly skipper Colin Cooter. Access to the dive boat is from the beach next to Selsey Lifeboat station where a tender collects divers and their kit. We found the boat spacious, more than comfortable and well equipped for the day's diving ahead of us. The wreck itself is around 50 minutes boat ride from the beach which gives you more than enough time to find a space, assemble your equipment and relax with a cup of tea. The dive itself is superb with around ten metres of visibility on a neap tide in 22 metres of water. The wreck being partially buried in the sand seabed, offers the chance to pocket a few scallops for tea. Plenty of bib and wrasse inhabit the wreck, which sank in 1918 on its way to Bombay after finding itself at the wrong end of a WW1 torpedo. It is also said that the remains of several 200lb bombs still lie about the wreck, but we didn't discover any on this occasion. Diving from this boat means you will be treated to a packed lunch courtesy of the crew and the chance of a second local dive to complete the day.

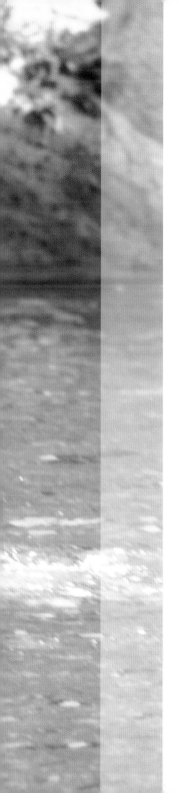

I want to go diving!

Firstly, if you haven't already, you will need to gain a basic diving qualification with a recognised agency. PADI's (Professional Association of Diving Instructors) "Open Water Diver" course is one route. You will learn the practical and theory elements with an instructor in the class room, swimming pool then four qualifying open water dives. Once qualified to this level you will be able to dive to a maximum depth of 18 metres. Independent dive centres and shops up and down the country and indeed the world over embrace the PADI way of learning dive. A quick Internet search will reveal the nearest PADI centre to you.

BSAC (British Sub Aqua Club), offer the "Ocean Diver" qualification with a BSAC instructor, combining class room work with confined water dives, then five open water dives. This qualification will allow you to dive to a maximum depth of 20 metres. See both PADI & BSAC websites for further reading and a comprehensive list of each qualifications benefits and limitations.

Once qualified, it is time to gain experience and explore some of the other courses on offer in order to increase your knowledge and confidence in diving. Further training will take you deeper and help you gain experience with a variety of challenging and exciting underwater environments.

If you are already qualified and just want to get into the water, simply book yourself on with one of the dives suggested in this book and you will be taken care of. It might be that you do not have a regular dive partner yet – no problem, let the dive centre know and they will often buddy you up with someone on the day. Local clubs organise regular UK diving trips and may be able to hire you equipment or assist with transport. Check out some of the Internet forums, where you will often see a "buddy finder" page, leading you to a like-minded diver in need of an underwater companion.

Ultimately, wherever you dive have great fun doing it and do it within your limits.

Useful dive centre & boat charter contacts

CORNWALL

Cornish Fishing
(Hard boat MV Wave Chieftain)
Diving for the Falmouth area
Skipper Nigel Hodge
www.cornishfishing.co.uk
Tel: 07976 974 616

Porthkerris Divers
Porthkerris Cove
St Keverne
Cornwall
TR12 6QJ
www.porthkerris.com
Tel: 01326 280620

DEVON

Clovelly Charters
(Lundy Island Dive Sites)
Skipper Clive Pearson
www.clovelly-charters.co.uk
Tel: 01237 431405
(Evenings 07774 190359)

**Lundy Shore Office
(Info & bookings)**
The Lundy Shore Office
The Quay, Bideford
Devon
EX39 2LY
www.lundyisland.co.uk
Tel: 01271 863 636

Aquanauts Dive Centre
88 Vauxhall St
The Barbican
Plymouth
PL4 0EY
info@aquanauts.co.uk
Tel: 01752 228825

Obsession Boat Charters
Andrew Bengey
The Moorings, 3 Mount View
Ilfracombe
Devon
EX34 9PD
www.obsessionboatcharters.co.uk
Tel: 01271 866325 / 07971 462024

DORSET

Fathom and Blues Ltd
262 Portland Road
Wyke Regis
Weymouth
Dorset
DT4 9AF
www.fathomandblues.co.uk
Tel: 01305 766220 / 01305 826789

Scimitar Diving (postal address)
37 Grosvenor Road
Portland
Dorset
DT5 2BQ
*(Use Postcode DT5 1BD
for Satnav direction to their boat)*
www.scimitardiving.co.uk
Tel: 07765 326728

Underwater Explorers Ltd
15 Castletown
Portland
Dorset
DT5 1BD
www.underwaterexplorers.co.uk
Tel: 01305 824 555

Divers Down
The Pier
High Street
Swanage, Dorset
BH19 2AR
www.diversdownswanage.co.uk
Tel: 01929 423565 (Diving Season)
or 01929 423551 (Nov - March)

HAMPSHIRE

Triton Scuba
147 Highland Road
Southsea
Hampshire
PO4 9EY
www.tritonscuba.co.uk
Tel: 023 92 838 773

Wight Diver (Adventure College)

Boat leaves from Hayling Ferry

Pontoon Southsea (Portsmouth)

19 Fairway Business Centre

Portsmouth

Hampshire

PO3 5NU

www.wightdiver.co.uk

Tel: 023 9269 1414

Selsey Fish Trips

(Hard boat diving) – For Witterings,

Selsey & Hampshire dive sites.

Boat usually leaves from near

Selsey Lifeboat Station

Skipper - Colin Cooter

www.selsey-fish-trips.com

Tel: 07779 654 022

WEST SUSSEX

Wittering Divers

12 Oakfield Road

East Wittering

Chichester

West Sussex

PO20 8RP

www.witteringdivers.co.uk

Tel: 01243 672 031

Southern Coast Charters

Simon Bradburn

Boat usually leaves from Bracklesham

Bay or Selsey East Beach

www.southerncoastcharters.com

Tel: 07932 162 721

Mulberry Divers Ltd

9 Orchard Parade

Selsey

Chichester

PO20 0NS

www.mulberrydivers.co.uk

Tel: 01243 601 000

Will Appleyard lives and works in London but spends much of his free time under water – usually off the south coast at the weekends or exploring his favourite Thailand and Red Sea sites when he has more time. When he's not under the sea then he's usually on the surface in his sea kayak.

Special thanks to:
Dad (thank you for the inspiration), Aleutia "Pipsy" Edgar, Graham Wimble, Tim Berry, Rob Roslyn, Neil Vickers, Al Turner, Caroline Boysen, Simon Bradburn, Dale & Ron Spree, Jo Cole, Clive Robins, Nicola Saunders, Scott & Jace, Sam Miles, Sara Clark, Kevan Chippindall-Higgin, Wittering Divers, Mulberry Divers and Porthkerris Divers

www.divinguk.co.uk
will@divinguk.co.uk